Published by Creative Education and
Creative Paperbacks
P.O. Box 227, Mankato, Minnesota 56002
Creative Education and Creative Paperbacks
are imprints of The Creative Company
www.thecreativecompany.us

Design by The Design Lab
Production by Chelsey Luther
Printed in the United States of America

Photographs by Corbis (Marcus Armani/National
Geographic Society, Michael Kern/Visuals Unlimited,
Andrew McLachlan/All Canada Photos), Dreamstime
(Melinda Fawver, Photographerlondon), Getty Images
(Jen St. Louis Photography, Universal Images Group),
Shutterstock (Thomas Barrat, Narisa Koryanyong,
Tyler Miller, mycteria), SuperStock (Anthony Mercieca)

Library of Congress Cataloging-in-Publication Data
Riggs, Kate.
Hawks / Kate Riggs.
p. cm. — (Amazing animals)
Summary: A basic exploration of the appearance,
behavior, and habitat of hawks, the birds of prey
found worldwide. Also included is a story from folk-
lore explaining how the sun is carried by hawks.
Includes index.
ISBN 978-1-60818-490-3 (hardcover)
ISBN 978-1-62832-090-9 (pbk)
1. Hawks—Juvenile literature. I. Title. II. Series:
Amazing animals.
QL696.F32R544 2015
598.9'44—dc23   2013051254

CCSS: RI.1.1, 2, 4, 5, 6, 7; RI.2.2, 5, 6, 7, 10;
RI.3.1, 5, 7, 8; RF.1.1, 3, 4; RF.2.3, 4

First Edition
9 8 7 6 5 4 3 2 1

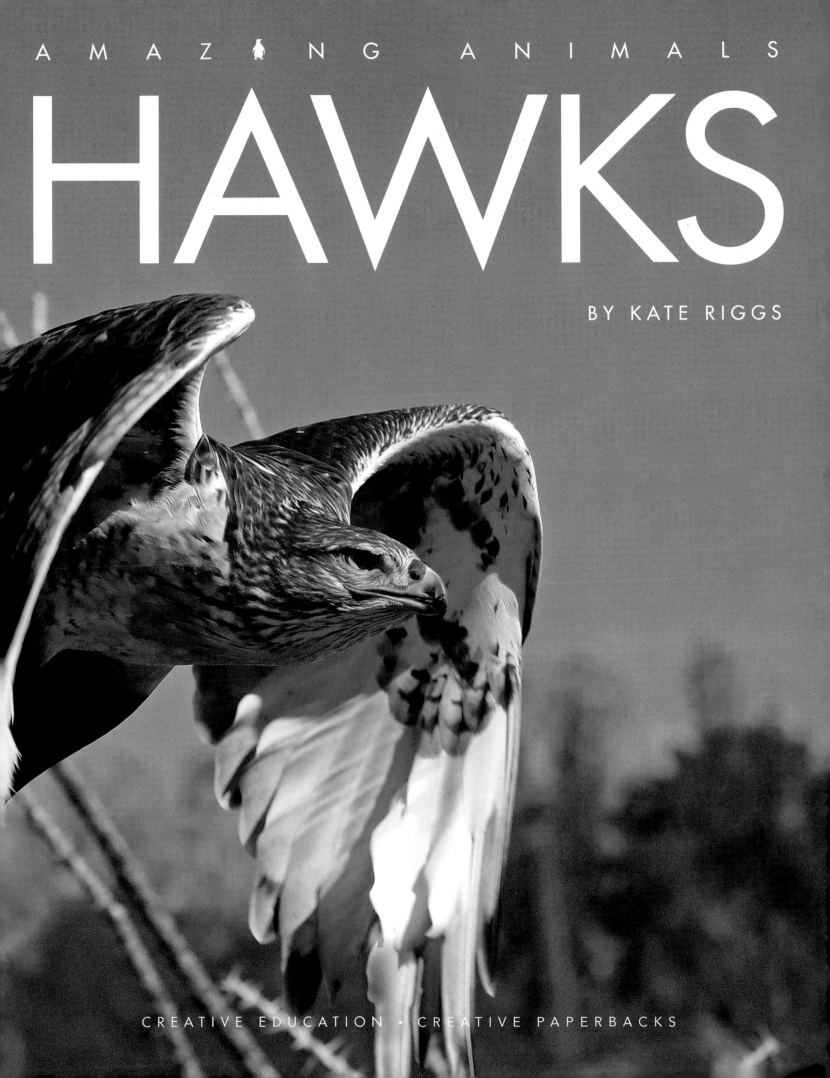

AMAZING ANIMALS

HAWKS

BY KATE RIGGS

CREATIVE EDUCATION · CREATIVE PAPERBACKS

Red-tailed hawks are common soaring hawks in North America

Hawks are **birds of prey** called raptors. There are more than 50 kinds of hawks. They are found all over the world. Some hawks are called "true" or forest hawks. Others are called broad-winged or soaring hawks.

birds of prey birds that hunt and eat other animals

*Hawks use their
talons to both catch
and kill their prey*

Soaring hawks have short tails and long wings. True hawks have long tail feathers and short wings. Hawks can see **prey** from far away. Like other raptors, hawks have curved beaks. They have sharp claws called talons, too.

prey animals that are killed and eaten by other animals

The largest and smallest hawks in the world live in North America. The ferruginous (*fih-ROO-jen-us*) hawk weighs up to five pounds (2.3 kg). Some sharp-shinned hawks weigh less than eight ounces (227 g).

Female ferruginous hawks are larger in size than males

Hawks that live in fields often fly close to the ground

Some hawks like open spaces, such as fields or **deserts**. Others live in hot, wet places around the world. Many hawks like to be near trees in a forest or by a river.

deserts hot, dry lands with little rainfall

Hawks hunt during the day. They look for mice, rabbits, and other animals. Hawks grab prey with their talons. Then they tear up meat with their beaks. If the meal is small enough, a hawk will swallow it whole.

Sometimes a hawk will take the fur off its prey before eating it

*Hawks are fed by
their parents until
they leave the nest*

A male hawk helps the female build a nest. Most kinds of hawks lay one to three eggs. The parents take turns keeping the eggs warm. **Hatchlings** come out of the eggs in 21 to 35 days. Newborn hatchlings are covered in white **down**. Feathers grow in over the next few weeks.

down the soft feathers of a young bird

hatchlings baby hawks

Red-tailed hawks can fly as fast as 120 miles (193 km) per hour

Young hawks learn how to hunt. They try to keep away from **predators**. Most hawks can live 12 to 16 years in the wild. Red-tailed hawks live about 21 years.

predators animals that kill and eat other animals

Some red-shouldered hawks fly to Mexico during the winter

Some hawks **migrate** to find food. They look for snakes, frogs, and other animals on the ground. Some hawks eat smaller birds.

migrate move from place to place during different parts of the year

Hawks like to sit in tall trees or on top of telephone poles. People can see them by a road or river. It can be exciting to see a hawk flying overhead!

Hawks can soar for hours on an upward flow of warm air

A Hawk Story

How does the sun go from east to west every day? People in Africa told a story about a hawk that carried the sun. A hawk and his human brother visited the ruler of the Land of the Sun. They wanted to bring the sun to the rest of the world. The king agreed, if the hawk promised to bring the sun back every night. So the hawk still holds the sun in his talons, going from the Land of the Sun out into the world every day.

Read More

Schaefer, Lola M. *Arrowhawk*. New York: Henry Holt, 2004.

Winter, Jeannette. *The Tale of Pale Male: A True Story*. Orlando: Harcourt/HMH Books for Young Readers, 2007.

Websites

San Diego Zoo Kids: Red-Tailed Hawk
http://kids.sandiegozoo.org/animals/birds/red-tailed-hawk
Learn more about red-tailed hawks.

Super Coloring: Hawks Coloring Pages
http://www.supercoloring.com/pages/category/birds/hawks/
Color pictures of hawks online or print them out.

Note: Every effort has been made to ensure that the websites listed above are suitable for children, that they have educational value, and that they contain no inappropriate material. However, because of the nature of the Internet, it is impossible to guarantee that these sites will remain active indefinitely or that their contents will not be altered.

Index